D0903529

The Thinking Girl's Treasury of Real Princesses

Isabella of Castile

Series editor **Shirin Yim Bridges**
Consulting editor **Amy Novesky**
Assistant writer **Lyndsey Jones**
Copy editor **Jennifer Fry**
Book design **Jay Mladjenovic**

Typeset mainly in Jane Austen and Volkswagen TS
Illustrations rendered in pen and watercolor

Manufactured in Singapore

Library of Congress PCN 2010903714

First Edition   10 9 8 7 6 5 4 3 2 1

Goosebottom Books LLC
710 Portofino Lane, Foster City CA 94404

www.goosebottombooks.com

For Tiegan and Alena, the original Thinking Girl
and the real Fairy-Monkey Princess.

~ Shirin Yim Bridges ~

For my family and friends.

~ Albert Nguyen ~

The Thinking Girl's Treasury of Real Princesses

Hatshepsut of Egypt

Artemisia of Caria

Sorghaghtani of Mongolia

Qutlugh Terkan Khatun of Kirman

Isabella of Castile

Nur Jahan of India

Isabella of Castile

By Shirin Yim Bridges | Illustrated by Albert Nguyen

goosebottombooks

She was called what?!

The Spanish princess and prince in this book were named Isabel and Fernando. In English, there is a long tradition of referring to them by their Italian names, Isabella and Ferdinand. If you want to search for more information about them online or in libraries, you'll find more using their Italian names, so those are the names used in this book.

Here, also, are some of the more unusual words in this book, with a rough-and-easy guide to pronunciation. You can hear many of the words pronounced on the website www.howjsay.com.

(Try it, it's neat.)

Castile	cas•teel
Segovia	seh•go•vee•ah
Tanto	tahn•toe
Monta	mon•tah
Grenada	gren•ah•dah
Conquistador	con•kwis•tah•door
Verdugado	vur•doo•gah•doe
Farthingale	far•thing•gale
Kirtle	ker•tel

Isabella of Castile

Have you ever noticed how in fairy tales, most princesses wait around to be rescued by a prince? Then they get swept away to a "happily ever after." They ride off into the sunset, and into a charmed life of fabulous palaces, beautiful clothes, and servants attending to their every need.

Well, for Isabella of Castile, being a princess was very different. As a little girl, Isabella lost her father and watched her mother lose her mind. She was exiled to a remote castle. Her childhood was sad and lonely. As she grew up, her country was divided by war. Despite all this, Isabella did find a "happily ever after." Or, to be more accurate: she made one for herself.

Isabella didn't wait to be found by a prince, she chose one. But before she married him, she made a deal that was completely revolutionary for her time. And, this remarkable princess, one of the most important in all of world history, has had an effect on your life. If it weren't for Isabella, Spain would not be the country it is today, and America would not exist as we know it!

Where she lived

When Isabella was born, Spain was not one country as we think of it today, but was divided into several kingdoms — Castile, Aragon, Navarre, and Grenada. For hundreds of years, these kingdoms were independent of each other, and often at war. One major cause of their fighting was religion. Castile, Aragon, and Navarre were all Christian kingdoms. Grenada was ruled by Muslims from North Africa, called the Moors.

When she lived

This timeline shows when the other princesses in The Thinking Girl's Treasury of Real Princesses once lived.

1500BC	500BC	1200AD	1300AD	1400AD	1600AD
Hatshepsut of Egypt	Artemisia of Caria	Sorghaghtani of Mongolia	Qutlugh Terkan Khatun	Isabella of Castile	Nur Jahan of India

Her story

Isabella was born in 1451. When she was just three years old, her father died, and her older half-brother, Henry, became King of Castile. Henry immediately sent Isabella's family away to a remote castle. Until Henry had a child, Isabella's brother, Alfonso, and Isabella herself were first and second in line for the throne. Henry did not want them at court where disgruntled nobles could use them in plots against him. So, for most of her childhood, Isabella lived in the small town of Arevalo. There, Isabella's mother withdrew into silence. Rumors flew that the exiled queen had gone mad. Still a child, Isabella sought comfort in books. It was a lonely existence.

But, things changed when Isabella turned 13. Henry was a weak and unpopular king. And even though Alfonso was no longer first in line for the throne (by now Henry had a daughter), many people put their hopes in the prince. Soon the country was torn by civil war between those who supported Henry and those who wanted to replace him with Alfonso. No end was in sight, and then Alfonso unexpectedly died. The people turned to Isabella. She could have continued the war hoping to grab the throne for herself, but she settled for being named heir to Castile. The quiet teenager from the faraway castle was now second only to the King.

Ferdinand of Aragon, King of Castile, of Aragon, and eventually of a reunited Spain. This portrait was probably painted shortly after his death.

Even as heir to the throne of Castile, a princess' role was to be a pawn in the marriage game. Their husbands were chosen for them by their families for purely political reasons, and once married, even if they inherited the throne, they were expected to be completely obedient to their husbands. Henry presented Isabella with many possible suitors, but against accepted behavior, she refused them all. She wanted to marry Ferdinand, heir to the throne of Aragon. Isabella knew that this marriage would unite the Kingdoms of Castile and Aragon into a unified Spain that would be a strong European power. (It's not very romantic, but in those days, marriages were much like business contracts.)

Henry would not allow the marriage. He was afraid that it would make Isabella too powerful. He soon learned that when Isabella made up her mind, there wasn't much anyone could do to change it. Isabella disobeyed her brother and negotiated a marriage with Ferdinand. The two met for the first time in secret, only days before their wedding. In the middle of the night, Ferdinand slipped into Isabella's palace by a back gate. He found the princess waiting for him, 18 years old and golden-haired, in a great room lit by torches. They spoke for hours. Their attraction was instant, mutual, and passionate — and would last throughout the years. They had met to make a political alliance, but Isabella and Ferdinand had fallen in love.

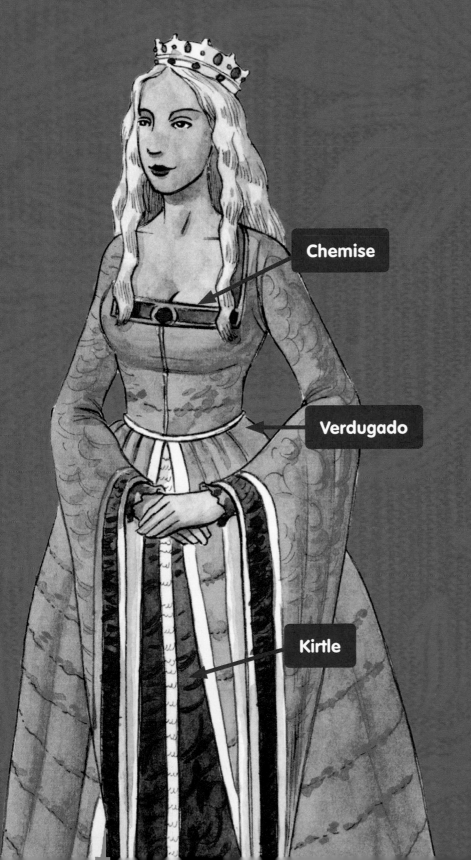

Chemise

Verdugado

Kirtle

What she wore

During Isabella's reign, an over-gown called the verdugado with a bell-shaped hoop skirt and long hanging sleeves became popular. This fashion spread across Europe and was known as the farthingale. Elizabeth I of England was still wearing farthingales 100 years later. Under the verdugado, Isabella would have worn a richly decorated under-gown, called a "kirtle," which often showed through at the neck, sleeves, and skirt. And under the kirtle, she wore a linen chemise, which fitted close to her body. On her head, Isabella often wore a jeweled crown or a small cap.

▲ You can still see Isabella's crown and Ferdinand's sword in the Royal Chapel at Granada.

Even so, Isabella insisted on an agreement before the marriage (similar to the modern "pre-nup"). This agreement made it very clear that she would keep her authority when she became Queen, and that Castile would be treated as more important than Aragon. Ferdinand promised to live in Castile and raise his children there, sign everything jointly, and share all titles.

In 1474, Henry died and Isabella was declared Queen of Castile in a ceremony that was literally fit for a king. To the blast of trumpets, she entered the church of San Miguel in Segovia to pray. Then, taking up a Castilian flag hanging from a lance, she placed it into the hands of the priest, signaling that she was offering herself and her kingdom to God. She left the church in a grand procession, riding on a horse under a canopy of state carried by the greatest nobles walking beside her. Preceding her was a single horseman, his right arm raised. In his hand was a naked sword, held by the point with the hilt up so that it looked like a cross. This was the symbol of royal authority — of the power to dispense punishment and justice. Until that moment, it was a symbol that had been reserved only for kings.

There was only one thing missing from Isabella's victorious day: Ferdinand. Isabella's coronation had occurred without his knowledge or presence. In her mind, she had inherited the throne, and it was only natural and right to immediately confirm the fact. She saw herself as the new sovereign, the dispenser of punishment and justice, worthy of being preceded by the sword.

When Ferdinand learned of Isabella's coronation, he was surprised that she had not waited for him. But he was most upset when he heard about the naked sword. What queen, he asked his counselors, had ever been preceded by the sword? Was it not the exclusive right of kings?! His Aragonese nobles, who (like Ferdinand!) might not have taken Isabella's pre-nup seriously enough, had no option but to agree that Isabella had broken all tradition by taking this sign of kingship for herself.

This gloomy portrait is said to have been painted in 1469 to celebrate Isabella and Ferdinand's wedding. Isabella is shown with surprisingly dark hair. Ferdinand's expression is a little easier to explain. As you know, he had plenty to sulk about that year!

What followed was a stormy time for Isabella and Ferdinand. Although at first the couple were just happy to be in love and united, the reality was that they had very different ideas about who would rule Castile. Isabella saw Castile as her inheritance alone. Ferdinand's power would come from her, because she was willing to share her power with him. Ferdinand, who came from a country where women were not legally allowed to rule, assumed that he would rule Castile despite formalities like sharing titles, quite simply because he was the man. (In those days, most of the world would have agreed with him.) Several times he was so offended by the reality of sharing power that he threatened to return to Aragon.

▲ Isabella and Ferdinand's thrones, with their motto "tanto monta" above.

Eventually, Isabella and Ferdinand came to an agreement. Instead of worrying about whose name would appear first, they would use one seal. They created a new joint coat of arms. They minted new coins with both of their portraits. And they came up with a new motto: "Tanto monta, monta tanto, Isabel como Fernando" — "To stand as high, as high to stand, Isabella and Ferdinand." It was a revolutionary moment in history: the first formally equal joint rule. And by 1479, when Ferdinand inherited the throne of Aragon, he had come to like this partnership with his wife enough to voluntarily make Isabella joint ruler of Aragon, too. (Here's a clue as to how revolutionary this equality really was: almost 100 years later, Isabella's granddaughter, Mary I of England, was still expected to give up her authority to her husband. This expectation that the man would rule even though the woman had inherited the throne was so strong that Mary's half-sister, Elizabeth I, refused to marry at all so that she could rule herself and England!)

▶ A document bearing their joint seal and both signatures.

▲ "Home" for Isabella and Ferdinand:
   the castle of Segovia.

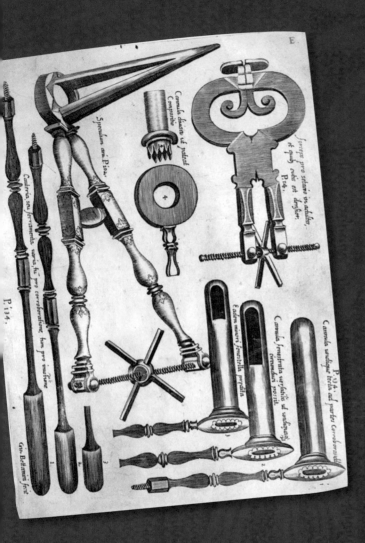

Surgical instruments from the 1500s. Isabella's doctors probably used very similar (and similarly frightening) tools!

With this difficult period behind them, Isabella and Ferdinand turned their sights outward. They began to plan the overthrow of Grenada that would reunite all of Spain. The same princess who had decided to wait for the throne in order to spare her country more civil war now prepared for a bloody conflict because she believed it was just.

Maybe as a gesture to soothe his recently ruffled ego, Isabella took a step back and let Ferdinand lead the war. She quietly made sure that everything ran smoothly behind the scenes. (Isabella may have been stubborn when it came to defending her authority, but she was always a sensitive and loving wife, and was not above sewing Ferdinand's shirts herself.)

However, as the war dragged on, Isabella became more physically involved. She recognized the need for medical aid on the front lines, and bravely took doctors and supplies there herself, setting up tents in the battlefield that became known as the "Queen's Hospitals." She also led the Castilian army in person, wearing armor and mounted on a warhorse. Finally, in 1492, Isabella and Ferdinand were victorious. After 781 years of Moorish rule, Grenada surrendered.

In *The Capitulation of Granada* (Francisco Pradilla y Ortiz, 1882) the Moorish ruler of Granada, Boabdil, surrenders the city to Isabella and Ferdinand.

What she ate

Before Columbus discovered America with Isabella's backing, the staples you would have found on Isabella's table were olives, olive oil, and wine (popular since ancient Greek and Roman times), meat, and fish. Many of the ingredients that are now so key to Spanish cooking — tomatoes, potatoes, and peppers — were only available and included in Spanish cuisine after the discovery of the New World!

Isabella and Ferdinand's reign is still thought of as Spain's Golden Age. First by their marriage, and then by their reconquest of Grenada, they had reunited the country. As Isabella had wanted all along, Spain was now a major European power. Then, by a stroke of daring and good fortune, Spain became an enormously rich empire.

During the war, a sailor named Christopher Columbus had come to Isabella, asking her to fund a risky expedition. He believed he could find a new route to Asia. No one else believed the venture would work — not even Ferdinand — but Isabella thought it was a gamble worth taking. She agreed to finance Columbus' expedition. A new route to Asia would have allowed Spain to trade directly with the East. Until then, all trade had passed through the Mediterranean, controlled (and heavily taxed) by the Genoans and Venetians.

The journey wasn't easy, nor did it go as planned, but it was a success. As you probably already know, Columbus didn't find a new route to Asia. Instead, he discovered what is today the Americas. He returned with great riches from the new world, surprising those who had doubted him, and making his supporter, Isabella, wealthy beyond imagination. The infamous Spanish conquistadors followed in his wake. Their brutal conquests made the Spanish empire the largest and richest in the western world. The European settlement of the new continent soon followed. If you live in North or South America, everything now outside your window would probably look very different if it weren't for this quiet and bookish princess.

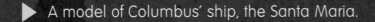

▶ A model of Columbus' ship, the Santa Maria.

The not-so-nice part of the story

Historians often use words like "principled" and "pure of heart," to describe Isabella. But there's another side to the coin. Under Isabella's rule, in her effort to drive out the Moors and reunite Spain, thousands of people were killed. (The Moors had been settled in Grenada for nearly 800 years. That's almost twice as long as Europeans have now been settled in the United States.)

Even after the war was over, Isabella was the driving force behind the infamous Spanish Inquisition. A reunited Spain was not enough. The country had to be united in Catholicism. Thousands of people, both Muslims and Jews, were forced to give up their religion or to flee their homes. Hundreds who stayed behind and were suspected of not being true converts were burned.

And, of course, the effect of the Spanish conquest of the Americas was just as bloody for its original inhabitants. Across the globe, many paid a high price for Isabella's successes. As the book about Artemisia in this series also shows, what's right or wrong can be a complex decision for princesses.

Her personal tragedy

Nothing brought Isabella greater joy, and eventually greater heartbreak, than her children. They were born heirs to all of Spain, but none had a long and happy life.

- Isabella (1470-1498) — Married first to Alfonso, Prince of Portugal, then to Manuel I of Portugal. Died at the age of 28 during childbirth.

- John, Prince of Asturias (1478-1497) — Married Archduchess Margaret of Austria, then died of tuberculosis at the age of 19 shortly after their marriage.

- Joanna "The Mad" (1479-1555) — Married Philip "The Handsome" of Burgundy. Her obsession with her husband — which was not mutual — and then his death, drove her to insanity. She had to be locked up by her father, King Ferdinand.

- Maria (1482-1517) — Married Manuel I of Portugal after her sister's death. Died at the age of 35.

- Catherine (1485-1536) — Married first to Arthur, Prince of Wales, then to his younger brother who became Henry VIII of England. Henry had their marriage scandalously annulled so that he could marry Anne Boleyn. Catherine died in poverty and lonely isolation.

- Peter (1488-1490) — Died at the age of 2. (No portrait available.)

Isabella died in 1504, and Ferdinand in 1516. They now lie side by side in the Royal Chapel of Grenada, the city they had fought so hard to win.